SNAP SHOT™

Art director Roger Priddy
Editor Mary Ling
Designer Joanna Pocock

SNAPSHOT™
an imprint of Covent Garden Books.
232 Madison Avenue,
New York, New York 10016

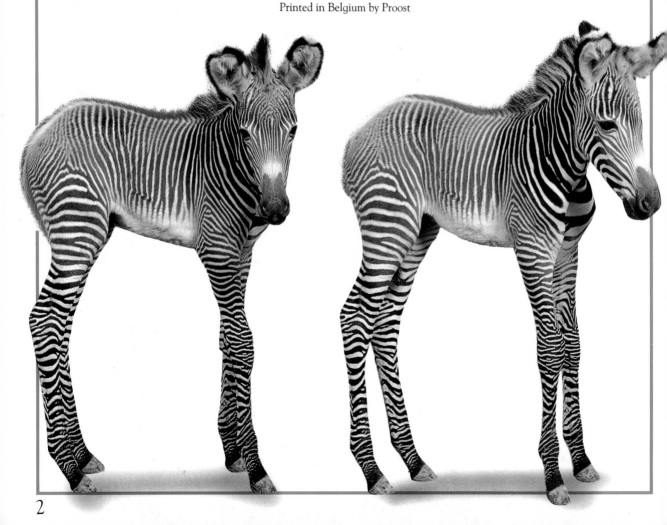

Funny Faces

Elephant

Contents

Spiny mouse

Is a pig's nose round?

A pig has a special round nose called a snout. It enjoys snuffling around in the mud for tasty things to eat.

Bloodhounds have sad faces—even when they are about to go for a walk.

Can a bloodhound smile?

Who hunts at night?

Owls do. Their sharp eyes
can see by moonlight.

What do monkeys see?

Monkeys
can see the
treetops as
they leap
from branch
to branch.

Why is this fish prickly?

This is a porcupine fish.
It puffs itself up to look really
big and scary to its enemies.

This horned frog loves eating. It lies in wait and gulps a tasty mouse meal in a flash.

Is this frog hungry?

This little frog makes its home in the trees of Australia. When the leaves rustle, it changes color. That's funny!

What's so funny?

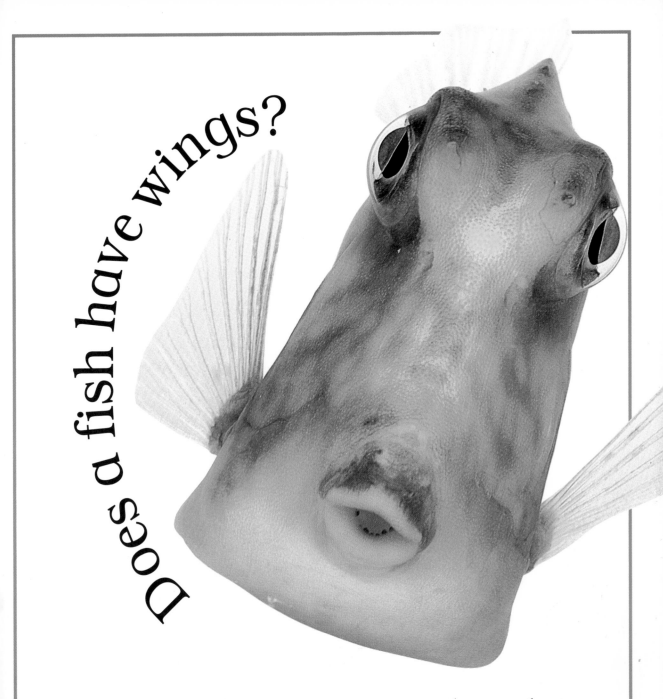

Does a fish have wings?

Fish have fins, not wings. The tail fin pushes the fish forward. The side fins steer it in the right direction.

Poodles' ears are not very big, but they are fluffy. Like all dogs, they can hear very well.

How big are my ears?

Who's squeaking please?

Marmosets squeak and whistle as they clamber through the jungles of Brazil.

What are whiskers for?

Whiskers measure spaces. They help cats feel their way through tight spots.

Where does this fox live?

This friendly fox lives in the Arctic. When snow falls, it grows white fur.

Bushbabies hunt at night. Their big eyes can see in the dark.

Do bushbabies stare?

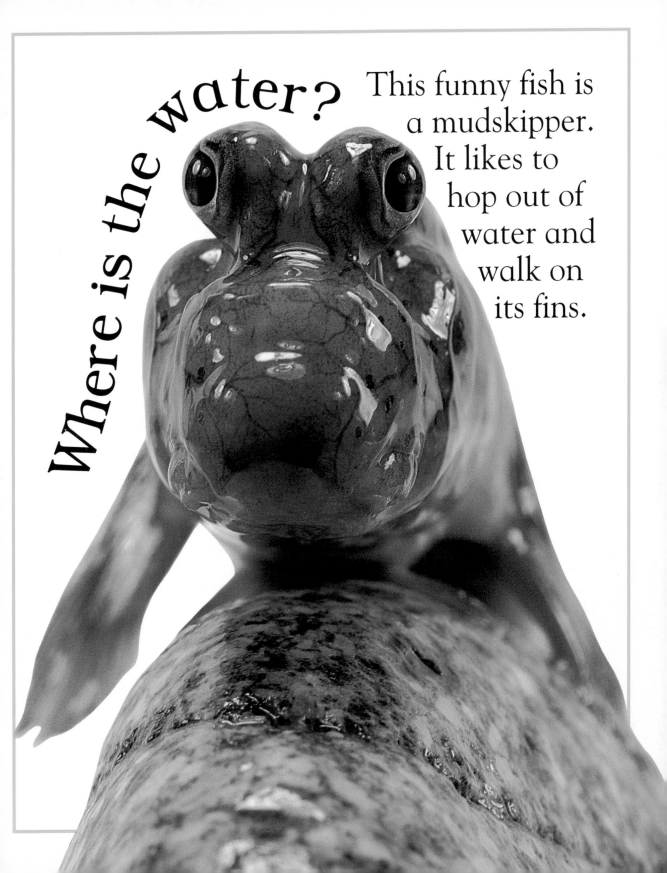

Where is the water?

This funny fish is a mudskipper. It likes to hop out of water and walk on its fins.

This is a caracal. It lives in Africa and Asia. Its short fur helps it keep cool in the heat.

What cat is this?

What dog is this?

It is
called a
Shar Pei.
It is very
wrinkly and
comes from
China.

How do ducks feed?

Ducks scoop plants off the surface of the water or tip upside down for food under the water.

What do cranes eat?

This crane's bill is perfect for catching quick insects.

Chimps love playing. It is their way of learning about life.

Who wants to play?

Orangutans spend most of their time eating fruit. They like sleeping, too.

What shall we eat?

The red-eyed tree frog hops from branch to branch in the rain-forest.

Can a frog fly?

A caiman cannot chew. If a meal is more than a mouthful, it tears off chunks with its sharp teeth.

Can a caiman chew?

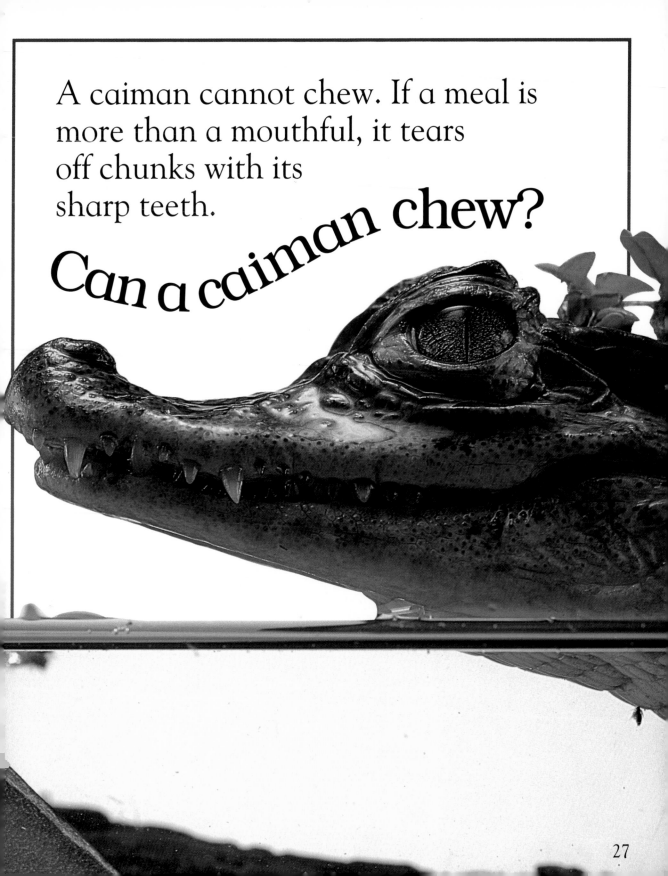

How long is this neck?

A giraffe's neck is long enough to nibble the tender green shoots high up in the treetops.

Can a zebra hide?

In a herd of zebras, it is hard to pick out just one because all the stripes mix together.

Faces come in many

Red-legged tortoise

Gouldian finch

Cane toad

Fruit bat

shapes and colors.

Harlequin
tusk fish

Patas
monkey